W9-AFA-637

> **EXTRA! EXTRA!**
> Planet Earth has about 1,500 active volcanoes, but not all of them are on land. Most are under the sea.

Scientists in a helicopter fly up close to an erupting volcano to study the explosion. Red-hot lava shoots into the sky, then trickles down the mountainside.

Angry Earth

Beneath its rocky crust, Earth is like a battle zone. Hot magma churns beneath the surface, and pressure builds up until the volcano is ready to blow. KA-POW!

A fountain of lava, gas, ash, dust, and rock spurts up.

Ready, Steady, Go!

A volcano begins when rocks inside the earth melt into magma. The magma collects into a huge blob called a magma chamber. Solid rock above pushes down on the magma and pressure builds up. If the rock cracks, the pressure is released. Gas bubbles may suddenly appear and magma shoots toward the surface and flies into the air as lava!

Magma explodes through a central hole, or vent.

Magma pours from vents

Layers of hardened lava and ash from old eruptions

Magma chamber deep underground

Earth's crust

ABT

FRIENDS OF ACPL

EXTRAORDINARY VOLCANOES

Contents

Allen County Public Library

A Big Bang!

If you see a mountain spitting fire, be ready to run. It's an exploding volcano! A violent volcanic eruption can be stronger than the most powerful bomb on earth!

Gush, Choke, Spew!

A volcano is an opening in the earth's surface. Most volcanoes are mountains, but others are just cracks in the ground. Some volcanoes gush fiery, liquid rock, called lava, while others spew out choking clouds of ash and gas. Other volcanoes do both!

Cough! Excuse me!

Dead or Alive?

Scientists describe volcanoes as active, dormant, or extinct. Active volcanoes bubble, getting ready to erupt or blow their tops. Dormant volcanoes are quiet but are expected to erupt again in the future. Extinct volcanoes have been sleeping for so long that they'll never erupt again — probably!

Wake me up when it's time to go!

Inside Story

To understand how a volcano happens, you need to know what's underneath your feet. Our planet is made up of several layers. The outer layer is a thin, rocky surface, called the crust. Beneath that is the mantle, a layer of molten, or melted, rock called magma (known as lava when it's aboveground). Next comes a layer of liquid metal called the outer core. At the center of the earth is the inner core, an incredibly hot ball of solid metal.

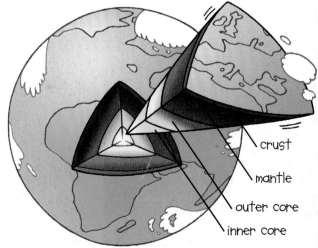

crust

mantle

outer core

inner core

Q. WHAT DO YOU CALL A CUTE VOLCANO?   A. LAVA-BLE!

HA HA

Huge lumps of lava, called volcanic bombs, are thrown out.

Jets of poisonous gas escape.

Mountain Maker

Each time a volcano erupts, the lava it produces cools and hardens, creating a new layer of rock. Over a long period of time, the layers of rock form on top of one another. This is why volcanoes grow into mountains.

Hi, can we join you?

This lava flow has cooled and a crusty surface has formed on top. But underneath, the lava is still boiling.

5

Ash, Fire, and Mud

During very violent eruptions, killer clouds of ash and gas can roll menacingly downhill. Then the lava pours down the mountainside.

Rivers of Fire

Lava from a violent eruption is slow and sticky, creeping along at about 15 feet (5 m) or so a day. If a volcanic eruption is less violent, the lava is runny and flows more quickly. Even so, it rarely moves faster than 6 miles per hour (10 kmh). Lava isn't speedy, but it is fiery. It's four times as hot as your oven, in fact!

Murderous Mud

A volcanic mudflow is a thick soup of hot or cold mud. It forms when ash and rock from an erupting volcano mix with rain or river water, or with melted snow and ice. A mudflow can be as deadly as lava, drowning everything in its path.

TRUE STORY!

When Indonesia's Galunggung volcano blew its top in 1982, it nearly brought down a jumbo jet. Ash from the eruption stopped the engines and the plane plummeted. Luckily, the captain managed to restart the engines and make a safe landing.

EXTRA! EXTRA!
An ash-and-rock cloud can travel as fast as a speeding car. That's at an incredible 120 miles per hour (193 kmh)!

Killer Cloud

In most eruptions, ash mixed with shattered chunks of volcanic rock shoots high in the sky. Sometimes this dangerous cloud rolls down the outside of the volcano at top speed, like a scorching avalanche. The ash cloud sweeps everything away, including trees, homes, and people. This is the deadliest of all volcanic blasts!

Too much ash...let's dash!

Billowing black clouds spell danger. This volcano in Papua New Guinea is active and pouring out ash clouds!

Drifting and Shifting

The ground beneath your feet may feel rock solid, but it isn't. Earth's crust is made up of about 20 vast pieces called plates. They are moving all the time, but so slowly that you can't feel it!

EXTRA! EXTRA!

Is it a moonscape? No, it's a volcanic landscape on the island of Java, Indonesia. It formed when new volcanoes bubbled up in the remains of an old one!

This spectacular volcanic landscape on the island of Java formed along the boundary lines between two plate edges. Many volcanoes erupt on the edges of plates.

Push and Shove

The earth's plates move because they float on the liquid mantle beneath the earth's solid crust. At some points, the plates push against each other, while at others they move apart. The earth's plates are moving between roughly 1 and 8 inches (2 and 20 cm) per year, which is about the same rate that your fingernails grow!

Bubble and Boil

Violent volcanoes are found at the edges of plates that push against each other. Quieter volcanoes erupt in the middle of plates and where plates are moving apart. Most of the world's really violent volcanoes lie in a circle around the plate edges, beneath and beside the Pacific Ocean. Life is so fiery and dangerous here that the region is called the Ring of Fire.

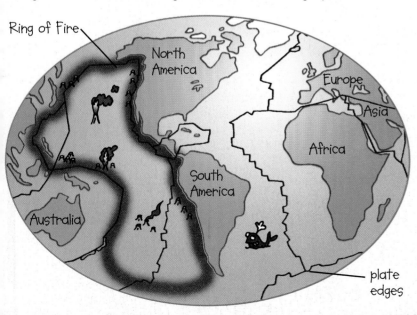

Break Away

1
About 240 million years ago, the separate pieces of land that we call the continents didn't exist. There was just one vast landmass, which we call Pangaea.

2
Over millions of years, the plates drifted and Pangaea slowly pulled apart. It broke up into smaller, separate landmasses that floated away from one another.

3
By around 45 million years ago, the continents had formed as we know them today. But they are still moving, little by little, year by year.

Islands of Fire

An underwater volcano usually bubbles away gently, oozing lava out over the seabed. Over thousands of years, it can grow from a little hump into a mountain, and even pop its head above water — as an island!

Rising Up from the Sea

Around the Pacific Ocean, long chains of islands have formed where two plates have collided. As the earth's crust was squeezed, a row of volcanic mountains was slowly pushed up above the surface.

Hot Hawaii

The Hawaiian Islands grew from volcanoes beneath the sea, but they formed in the center of a plate over a hot spot. This is an area beneath the earth's crust that is so hot that magma forms. The magma finds its way through cracks in the crust to form a volcano which, in time, grows above the waves.

Wow! What's tha

New Land, Ahoy!

1

In 1963, fishermen off the coast of Iceland thought they could see a boat on fire! But no, it was the tip of a steaming-hot new island.

Uh oh!

2

By nightfall, the new island was 35 feet (11 m) high. Today it's the size of a small city. It is called Surtsey, after a Viking fire god called Surt.

EXTRA! EXTRA!
Loihi is a new volcanic island growing near Hawaii. Don't set your heart on seeing it, though — it won't pop up out of the water for another 60,000 years!

You wouldn't want to lie on this Hawaiian beach — or go for a swim! Magma has bubbled into a stream of burning lava that flows into the sea, making the water steam and spit.

Lava Lovers

Q. WHAT'S A VOLCANOLOGIST'S FAVORITE KIND OF MUSIC?   A. ROCK MUSIC!

HA HA

▲ Too hot to handle! This person wears a protective suit and heat-resistant gloves to pick up a sample of red-hot lava. Luckily, the lava flow behind is the slow-moving kind!

Would you like to get dressed up sort of like an astronaut and collect lava samples? That's part of the job of a volcanologist — a scientist who studies why and how volcanoes erupt.

On the Job

Being a volcanologist is an exciting job. You might specialize in lava flows or jets of hot water, called geysers. Or you would study the chemistry of ancient volcanic rocks, or even volcanoes out in space. You would have the chance to get close to an active volcano, too. That would definitely be a thrill!

Early Warnings

Volcanologists keep tabs on active volcanoes. They try to predict when a volcano's going to blow, so that people nearby have time to escape. Instruments record danger signals that show the buildup of magma inside the volcano. For example, a bulge in a volcano's side is a sign that it may be about to blow.

That's Weird!

If you want your own personal volcano-warning system, watch your pets. People say that dogs go completely haywire before an eruption!

What
do volcanologists wear?

When they're working on a volcano, most volcanologists put on normal work clothes — jeans, boots, and a hard hat to protect them from flying rocks.

The going gets tough when a volcano is about to blow. The air fills with poisonous gases, so volcanologists cover their faces and wear gas masks.

When things really heat up, volcanologists wear protective suits. A shiny aluminum finish reflects heat, helping them to keep their cool.

City of Ash

In 79 A.D., more than 2,000 people died when Mount Vesuvius, a volcano in southern Italy, blew its top. A killer cloud of fiery ash and poisonous gas rolled down over the nearby Roman city of Pompeii.

Going, going...

Vesuvius is still active and is the most studied volcano in the world. It last erupted in 1944, when it destroyed a nearby village. In the 79 A.D. explosion, ash poured down on Pompeii for two days. The city was buried to a height of 23 feet (7 m), way above the rooftops!

...gone!

Soon after the eruption, it began to rain. The ash turned into mud, which then set hard like rock. For centuries, Pompeii lay buried. Then, in the 1700s, its secrets were revealed by archaeologists, who are people that study ancient remains. They dug their way into the city, putting together a picture of Roman life.

TRUE STORY!

The people of Pompeii loved scribbling on walls. People have uncovered all sorts of graffiti — including, "Successus the cloth-weaver loves Iris the innkeeper's slave girl"!

EXTRA! EXTRA!
At times during the eruption, the column of ash above Vesuvius may have been 20 miles (32 km) high! That's nearly four times the height of Mount Everest!

Everything at Pompeii was frozen in time, from the shapes of people's fallen bodies and half-eaten meals, to furniture and the painted walls of houses.

Plaster People

Over the years, the bodies of the dead Romans rotted away to leave body-shaped holes inside the rock. When archaeologists discovered these holes, they poured plaster into them and let it set. Then, they chipped away the surrounding rock. They were left with plaster models of the fleeing victims and even their pets!

Rocky Relics

As time goes by, lava from volcanic eruptions creates different kinds of rock. Runny lava can cool into extremely hard types of rock, such as basalt, while volcanic ash sets into a softer rock known as tuff.

That's Weird!

A volcanic rock called pumice forms from frothy lava. As the rock becomes solid, air is trapped inside it, making it light enough to float in water. Pumice is put in the wash with jeans. Its rough surface rubs the jeans and makes them look old, or stonewashed!

EXTRA! EXTRA! These crazy cones are made of tuff. Thousands of years of wind and rain have carved them into shape!

Wind and rain create all sorts of weird landscapes, including these bizarre volcanic rock cone in Ürgüp, Turkey. More than 1,500 years ago, people hollowed out the insides to make homes.

Crazy Paving!

The Giant's Causeway in Northern Ireland is made up of more than 40,000 strange stone pillars. It's called a causeway because some of the stones look as if they are stepping-stones across the sea. The pillars formed millions of years ago, when lava hardened into basalt.

Finn's Footpath

1 According to old stories, the Giant's Causeway was made by the giant Finn MacCool, a legendary Irish hero. Across the sea in Scotland, Finn had a rival, who was named Benandonner.

2 I'm comin' to getcha!

The giants shouted across the Irish Sea and challenged each other to a contest of strength. So Finn built a causeway of stepping-stones between the two countries, to make the contest possible!

True Blue

One of the U.S.A.'s most spectacular spots is the 6-mile-(10-km) wide Crater Lake, in Oregon. It formed after the Mount Mazama volcano blew its top nearly 7,000 years ago. The mountain collapsed inward, plugging the hole, or crater, that was left. The crater slowly filled with water to create a brilliant blue lake. A baby volcano grew in the middle of the lake!

Hi, Mom!

Q. WHERE'S A CAVEMAN'S FAVORITE PLACE TO SIT? A. A ROCK-ING CHAIR!

HA HA

Hot Stuff!

You've heard the bad news about volcanoes, but there is some good news, too. The stuff that comes out of a volcano can be put to good use — and it can be amazing to watch.

Monkey Business

In volcanic countries, such as New Zealand and Japan, heat from volcanic rocks warms underground water, making hot springs bubble. Natural outdoor pools form, where you can go for a warm swim, even in winter! High in the snowy mountain forests of Japan, the macaque monkeys bathe in hot springs to warm themselves up. Now, *that's* luxurious!

That's Weird!

A volcano is a great place to grow fruit and vegetables, especially if it's dormant! Since ancient times, the slopes of volcanoes have been farmed because the ash from old eruptions makes the soil rich in the chemicals that help plants grow.

Hey, great grapes!

Bathing Beauties

Sometimes, underground water mixes with soil to create warm mud pools. Many people believe that bathing in the mud can cure illnesses or make skin beautiful.

How

do hot rocks heat homes?

Iceland may sound chilly, but with over 200 volcanoes, things are hot underground. This natural power is called geothermal energy.

In some parts of Iceland, piping-hot underground water is channeled into homes for central heating.

In other countries, including Italy, New Zealand, and the U.S.A., geothermal energy is used to generate electricity for lighting and heating.

EXTRA! EXTRA!
Each time Castle Geyser erupts, there's a 20-minute spout of water, followed by 40 minutes of steam!

Volcanic heat causes geysers to erupt. This one is called Castle Geyser. It's in Yellowstone National Park.

Earthquake!

The ground quivers. Then it splits right open and a gaping hole appears in front of you. It's an earthquake! Like a volcano, an earthquake happens when the earth's plates shift.

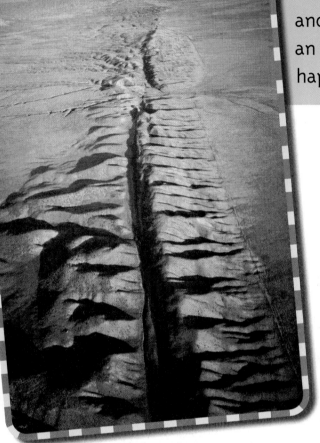

Whose Fault?

The earth shakes and quakes when the gigantic plates that make up its crust suddenly crack and move. An earthquake usually happens along a weakness in the crust, called a fault, such as the San Andreas fault in California. As the rock cracks, huge chunks of ground may drop down, shoot upward, or even scrape past each other in opposite directions. But most earthquakes are so slight that you might not even notice them!

What a Shock!

Shudders spread out from the center of an earthquake like the ripples from a stone thrown into a pond. These shudders are known as shock waves. Some shock waves roll across the earth's surface, while others race along deep under the ground.

After an earthquake, rescue workers hunt for survivors. This scene shows Mexico City in 1985.

How

do I survive an earthquake?

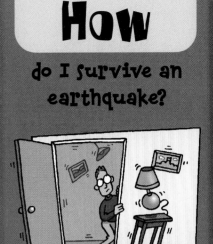

If you experience an earthquake, dive for cover. Hide under a table or in a doorway for protection from falling walls and ceilings.

During a quake, windows can shatter, outside walls crumble, and things fall off shelves. So take cover and keep away from them.

Never rush outdoors. Don't move until the shaking stops. Although earthquakes are scary, most of them are pretty minor.

Making Waves

A violent volcano or earthquake is bad enough on land, but if either of them happens at the bottom of the ocean, they can stir up a monstrous wave, known as a tsunami.

TRUE STORY!

In 1960, a tsunami set off on a marathon globetrotting trip! A gigantic earthquake struck off the coast of Chile, causing the tsunami to smash over the Chilean coast. Just 15 hours later, the tsunami had raced across the Pacific Ocean to Hawaii. Seven hours after that, it blasted Japan on the opposite side of the ocean!

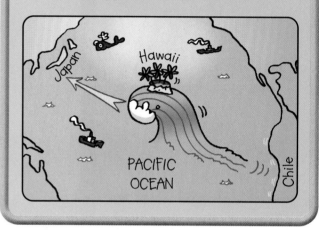

Wall of Water

A tsunami isn't all that high when it begins out at sea. But as the wave reaches the coast, it rears up into a vast wall that smashes over the land and sweeps away entire villages.

Pirates' Paradise

1 Ordinary people used to shiver when they heard the name Port Royal. This harbor town on the island of Jamaica was once a pirate haunt.

2 Port Royal was known as the worst city on earth until June 1692, when an earthquake triggered a gigantic tsunami.

3 Hundreds of people died, and the pirates' ships and the town's buildings were smashed to pieces. There was no more piracy for Port Royal!

Watery Wonders

Tsunamis happen on the surface, but there are other volcanic wonders on the seabed. Scientists send robot mini-submarines to study extraordinary natural chimneys, called black smokers. These are hot springs that form in the seabed where seawater seeps through cracks and is heated by the magma below. All sorts of weird creatures, such as red-and-white worms as long as cars, live in the hot water near the black smokers.

EXTRA! EXTRA!
Tsunami was originally a Japanese word, meaning "harbor wave"!

Imagine this arc of water bearing down on you! There's no time to get out of the way as the tsunami races across the ocean at over 500 miles per hour (800 kmh) — as fast as a jet plane.

Headline News

Most of us go about our daily lives giving little thought to the hidden world beneath our feet. But every now and then, something amazing happens that reminds us of the awesome power of the earth's natural forces.

Unstoppable!

How would you feel if your yard was invaded by a surging mass of burning lava? This event is common on Hawaii, which is one of the most volcanic places on Earth. Two Hawaiian volcanoes have erupted 77 times between them in the past 200 years — almost once every three years. One eruption lasted for a year and a half!

Rocketing Around the World

1 In 1883, the volcano on the island of Krakatau, Indonesia, exploded, making the noisiest eruption ever. It was heard across the ocean in Australia.

2 There were no people living on Krakatau, but the eruption stirred up tsunamis that smashed over nearby islands, causing huge destruction.

3 The ash from the explosion traveled so far around the world that it turned sunsets a spectacular red as far away as Europe.

Mount St. Helens, in Washington, lay dormant for 123 years. Then in 1980, it exploded. Ash and gas blasted out, flattening houses and trees for 19 miles (30 km).

Dark Skies

In 1991, Mount Pinatubo in the Philippines erupted. The explosion sent a gigantic cloud of ash and gas shooting 22 miles (35 km) up into the air. It blocked out the sun for days and the sky went dark. People, crops, and animals were caked in dust.

That's Weird!

The Mount St. Helens eruption created boiling-hot mudflows, which swept into nearby rivers, heating them and making fish leap out of the water!

HA HA

25

Space Oddities

Volcanoes exist in space — it's true! As well as Earth, there are other rocky planets and moons moving around our sun that have volcanoes. Like Earth, the surfaces of Venus and Mars were shaped by volcanoes and earthquakes. The volcanoes on Mars are now extinct, but scientists think that some of those on Venus are alive and kicking!

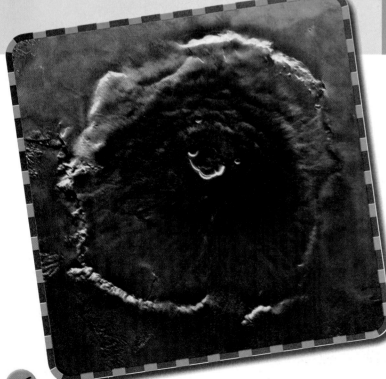

EXTRA! EXTRA!
One of Venus's volcanoes is an incredible 250 miles (400 km) across. That's almost as long as the Grand Canyon!

Rock Monster

The biggest volcano in the solar system is Olympus Mons on Mars. It's 16 miles (25 km) high and an amazing 440 miles (700 km) wide — that's wide enough to cover the entire state of Arizona. There are other gigantic volcanoes on Mars, too.

The Gas Planets

There are no volcanoes on Jupiter and the other gaseous planets because these planets don't have a rocky crust with melted magma beneath. But the gas planets do have rocky moons, and some of these moons have active volcanoes.

Exploding Pizza!

Io is one of Jupiter's 16 moons. It is the most spectacular moon in the solar system, with even more erupting volcanoes than Earth. And because its lava is colored by red, orange, and yellow chemicals, Io's surface looks a lot like a cheese-and-tomato pizza!

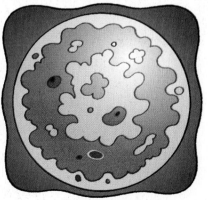

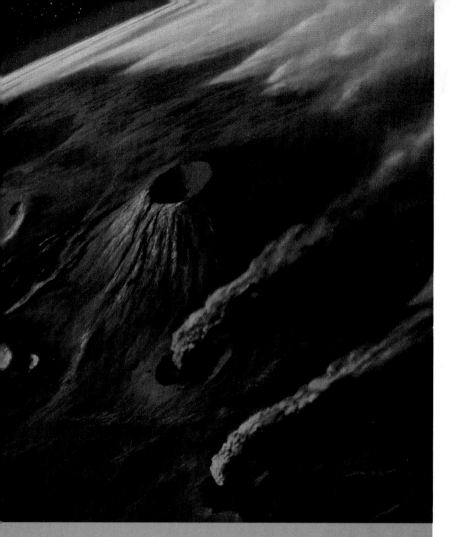

▲ The surface of Venus is full of volcanoes. Imagine smoke billowing from Venus's crater-filled, burning-hot face.

That's Weird!

There are no volcanoes on the moon, but in the past there were lava flows. These may have been caused by space rocks crashing onto the moon! The rocks may have smashed the crust, releasing molten rock from below. The lava flows created flat plains known as "seas," because that's what they look like from Earth.

No sea? No surf? Take me home!

Extra Amazing

Want to know the hot facts about volcanoes and earthquakes? Here are some of the top happenings from around the world, including a few legends from way back in ancient times.

Top Explosion

One way of measuring volcanoes is by the Volcanic Explosivity Index (VEI, for short). This grades eruptions from 0 (non-explosive) to 8 (mega-colossal). Fortunately, there haven't been any grade 8 eruptions for hundreds of thousands of years, and the last grade 7 eruption was on Tambora, Indonesia, in 1815.

Hawaiian Top Spots

Sparks are always flying on Hawaii! It's the home of Mauna Loa, one of the world's most active volcanoes. It is also the world's largest, covering over 2,000 square miles (5,200 square km). That's more than half of the island of Hawaii! Its dormant neighbor, Mauna Kea, is the world's tallest volcano. Measured from its base on the ocean floor, Mauna Kea is a whopping 32,000 feet (9,800 m). Side by side, it would be taller than Everest, the world's highest mountain!

Greatest Quake

An earthquake can be measured against a scale, called the Richter scale, which grades it according to how much energy it releases. The scale ranges from 1 (a slight tremor that you can't even feel) to 9 (a violent earthquake that causes major damage over a large region). The most powerful earthquake ever measured happened off the coast of Chile, in 1960. It reached 9.5 on the Richter scale.

It feels like a grade 3...

God of Fire

Since time began, people all over the world have told stories to explain the awesome power of volcanoes and earthquakes. The ancient Greeks believed that they were caused by Hephaestus, who was a blacksmith and god of fire and metalwork. Eruptions were sparks from his underground forge. The Romans renamed this god Vulcan. The modern word *volcano* comes from his name.

Pele Power

According to Hawaiian legends, volcanic eruptions and earthquakes were created by the goddess Pele. She stirred them up by digging into the ground with her magic stick and stamping with her feet.

Volcano Princess

The Aztecs were an ancient people who lived in Mexico. They told many legends about the volcanoes Popocatépetl and Ixtacihuatl. In one legend, Princess Ixtacihuatl killed herself when she was told that her suitor Popocatépetl was dead. He wasn't, and he vowed to watch over her forever. Even today, the Ixtacihuatl volcano looks like a woman lying down covered in a sheet of white snow, with Popocatépetl standing at her feet.

True or False?

Are you a volcanic whiz-kid? Test your knowledge and say whether each of these is true or false. Answers are on page 32, but no cheating!

1. All volcanoes are mountains.
2. All of Earth's volcanoes are underwater.
3. This is a picture of a dormant volcano.
4. Lava is solid rock.
5. Lava flows fastest from violent volcanoes.
6. Volcanic ash-and-gas clouds can travel as fast as a speeding car.
7. Earth's surface crust is solid.
8. Iceland is not volcanic.
9. Scientists who study volcanoes are called volunteers.

Volcano Terms

active volcano
A volcano that is either erupting now, or likely to do so in the near future.

crater
The bowl-shaped opening on top of a volcano, left by an eruption.

crust
Earth's rocky surface skin. The crust's thickness varies from about 4 to 25 miles (6 to 40 km).

dormant volcano
A volcano that hasn't erupted for a while, but may do so at some time in the future.

eruption
Lava, gas, and ash escaping onto the earth's surface. Eruptions range from spurts to explosions.

extinct volcano
A volcano that hasn't erupted for thousands of years and is unlikely ever to erupt again.

fault
A crack in the earth's crust.

geyser
A hot spring that, from time to time, spouts hot water and steam into the air.

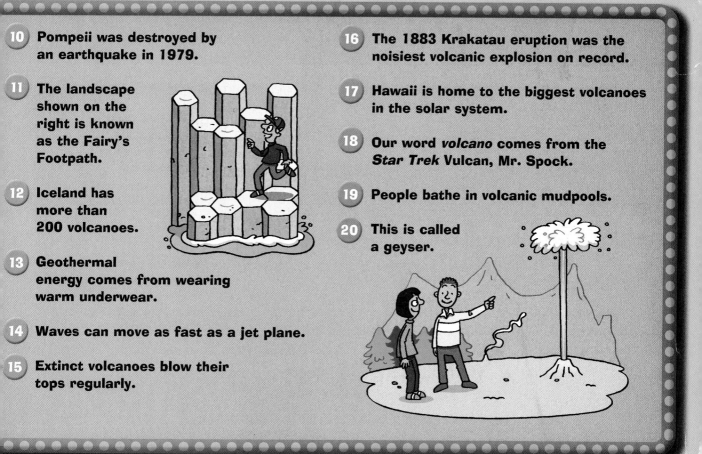

10 Pompeii was destroyed by an earthquake in 1979.

11 The landscape shown on the right is known as the Fairy's Footpath.

12 Iceland has more than 200 volcanoes.

13 Geothermal energy comes from wearing warm underwear.

14 Waves can move as fast as a jet plane.

15 Extinct volcanoes blow their tops regularly.

16 The 1883 Krakatau eruption was the noisiest volcanic explosion on record.

17 Hawaii is home to the biggest volcanoes in the solar system.

18 Our word *volcano* comes from the *Star Trek* Vulcan, Mr. Spock.

19 People bathe in volcanic mudpools.

20 This is called a geyser.

hot spot
A place beneath the earth's crust, where the mantle is hotter than normal. This creates magma, which may erupt at the surface to form a volcano.

lava
Hot, melted rock that erupts from a volcano.

magma
Hot, melted rock beneath the earth's surface.

mantle
The hot layer between the earth's surface and its central core.

mudflow
A river of mud that forms when earth and volcanic ash mix with water.

plate
One of 20 or so pieces that make up the earth's crust.

tsunami
A giant ocean wave, triggered by an undersea earthquake or volcanic eruption.

vent
An opening in a volcano, through which lava, gas, and ash escape.

volcanic ash
Tiny bits of dustlike rock and lava, which explode from volcanoes during eruptions.

volcano
An opening in the earth's crust, through which lava, gas, and ash may erupt.

Index

Answers

1 False	11 False
2 False	12 True
3 False	13 False
4 False	14 True
5 False	15 False
6 True	16 True
7 True	17 False
8 False	18 False
9 False	19 True
10 False	20 True

Author: Jackie Gaff
Illustrations: Andrew Peters; pp. 4-5 Julian Baum.
Consultant: Rodney Walshaw, BSc, PhD
Photographs: Cover: James A. Sugar/CORBIS; p. 3 Douglas Peebles/CORBIS; p. 5 Roger Ressmeyer/CORBIS; p. 6 Francois Gohier/Ardea London; p. 7 Tammy Peluso/Oxford Scientific Films; p. 8 Pacific Stock/Bruce Coleman; p. 10 Amos Nachoum/CORBIS; p. 11 Brenda Tharp/The Stock Market; p. 12 Roger Ressmeyer/CORBIS; p. 14 Alberto Nardi/NHPA; p. 15 Bettman/CORBIS; p. 16 Elio Ciol/CORBIS; p. 17 Michael Brooke/Oxford Scientific Films; p. 18 Jean-Paul Ferrero/Ardea London; p. 19 Bruce Coleman Inc.; p. 20 Tony Stone Images; pp. 20-21 Francois Gohier/Ardea London; p. 23 Tony Stone Images; p. 24 Francois Gohier/Ardea London; p. 25 Gary Braasch/CORBIS; p. 26 Tony Stone Images; pp. 26-27 Astrofoto/Bruce Coleman; p. 28 Pacific Stock/Bruce Coleman.

Created by act-two for Scholastic Inc. Copyright © act-two, 2001
All rights reserved. Published by Scholastic Inc.

SCHOLASTIC and associated logos are trademarks and/or registered trademarks of Scholastic Inc.

No part of this publication may be reproduced in whole or in part, or stored in a retrieval system, or transmitted in any form or by any means, electronic, mechanical, photocopying, recording, or otherwise, without written permission of the publisher. For information regarding permission, write to Scholastic Inc., Attention: Permissions Department, 555 Broadway, New York, NY 10012.

ISBN 0-439-28725-1

12 11 10 9 8 7 6   3 4 5 6/0

Printed in the U.S.A.

First Scholastic printing, September 2001